TO THE
PRECIOUS BLOOD

"Thou art worthy, O Lord, to take the book, and to open the seals thereof; because thou wast slain, and hast redeemed us to God, in thy blood, out of every tribe, and tongue, and people, and nation." —Apocalypse 5:9

The Sacred Heart is the Divine Chalice
overflowing with the Precious Blood
for the relief of the souls in Purgatory.

DEVOTION
TO THE
PRECIOUS BLOOD

INCLUDING PRAYERS
TO THE PRECIOUS BLOOD

"Knowing that you were not redeemed with corruptible things as gold or silver . . . but with the precious blood of Christ, as of a lamb unspotted and undefiled."
—1 Peter 1:18-19

TAN BOOKS AND PUBLISHERS, INC.
Rockford, Illinois 61105

Nihil Obstat: Philippus
                  Abbas Neo-Angelo Montanus

Imprimatur: ✛ Franciscus
                  Episcopus Sancti Josephus

Originally published by the Benedictine Convent of
Perpetual Adoration, Clyde, Missouri. 6th Edition,
1926.

ISBN-13: 978-0-89555-880-0
ISBN-10: 0-89555-880-7

Cover image: detail of "The Crucifixion" stained-glass
window. Photo © 1995 by Alan Brown, Bardstown,
Kentucky.

Printed and bound in the United States of America.

TAN BOOKS AND PUBLISHERS, INC.
P.O. Box 424
Rockford, Illinois 61105
2008

"Father, if thou wilt, remove this chalice from me: but yet not my will, but thine be done. And there appeared to him an angel from heaven, strengthening him. And being in an agony, he prayed the longer. And his sweat became as drops of blood, trickling down upon the ground." —*Luke* 22:42-44

"But after they were come to Jesus, when they saw that he was already dead, they did not break his legs. But one of the soldiers with a spear opened his side, and immediately there came out blood and water." —*John* 19:33-34

"Drink ye all of this. For this is my blood of the new testament, which shall be shed for many unto remission of sins."
—*Matthew* 26:27-28

Contents

O Jesu Lord,
Unclean I am, but cleanse me
   in Thy Blood,
Of which a single drop
   for sinners spilt,
Can purge the entire world
   from all its guilt.
   —From the *Adoro Te Devote*

Chapter 1

Devotion to the Precious Blood

VENERATION of the Precious Blood of our Lord Jesus Christ is a devotion as old as our Holy Faith. This Precious Blood, by which mankind was to be redeemed, was alluded to immediately after the Fall of our first parents in the Garden of Paradise.

God Himself ordained the burnt offerings and sacrifices of propitiation of the pre-Christian era, whereby, for four thousand years, the blood of animals was to be shed and offered as a sign of the honor due to Him.

The object of these sacrifices was likewise to keep alive and to transmit to posterity the faith in the promised Messias who was to redeem the world by the shedding of His Blood, to implant love for the Anointed One in the hearts of His chosen

1

people, and to enliven their hope.

The Precious Blood of our Redeemer was prefigured by the innocent blood of Abel, by the sacrifices of Isaac and Melchisedech, by the Paschal Lamb (the blood of which was sprinkled on the doorposts of the ancient Israelites on the night before they left Egypt), by the blood of innocent animals in the Old Covenant, and by many other customs practiced by the Israelite people. The prophecies—and the prophets to whom God showed in spirit when, where and in what manner it was to be shed— had reference to this Blood which Our Lord would shed in His Passion to redeem us. This is the Blood of the New and Eternal Testament, from which all the Sacraments derive their efficacy, from which all graces proceed, and from which, like heavenly dew, all graces are **ever descending upon the children of God.**

The Precious Blood is being daily consecrated and offered by priests in the Mass, and it is at all times venerated by the faithful in the Most Blessed Sacrament of the Altar. In Holy Communion, **all receive the Flesh and Blood of Jesus Christ** as a pledge of life eternal. True Catholics must venerate the Precious Blood of Jesus Christ unto the End of the World.

Venerators of the Precious Blood

Who have been the great venerators of the Precious Blood? St. Peter said to the Christians, "You were not redeemed with corruptible things, as gold or silver . . . but with the precious blood of Christ, as of a lamb unspotted and undefiled." (*1 Peter* 1:18-19). In his epistles, St. Paul wrote most beautifully on the Precious Blood. To the Colossians he writes: "And through him to reconcile all things unto himself, making peace through the blood of his cross . . ." (*Colossians* 1:20). St. John the Evangelist magnificently extols the Precious Blood; and in the *Apocalypse,* when he beholds the great multitude standing before the throne of God, he tells us: "These are they who are come out of great tribulation and have washed their robes and have made them white in the blood of the Lamb." (*Apocalypse* 7:14). St. Augustine was accustomed to turn his eyes toward the bleeding wounds of Jesus and say: "Lord, Thou bearest me, written in Thy hands, in ineffaceable characters, which are Thy most holy wounds; and to

inspire me with confidence, Thou gently say-
est: 'I have written thee in My hands with
the marks of My most holy wounds . . .'
Therefore will I ever say to Thee: 'Read, Lord
Jesus, read that handwriting and save me
through Thy Precious Blood.'"

Toward two devotions St. Augustine was
powerfully drawn; for two objects he had
the deepest reverence: **Our bleeding, crucified Saviour,** and Mary nourishing her
Divine Child. He was accustomed to say:
"Each time when I behold my Crucified
God, I am filled with confidence and love,
but I must confess that I experience the
same sentiments, in the same degree, when
I contemplate the thrice-blessed breasts
which gave nourishment to the Son of God.
Placed between these two heavenly objects,
I indeed know not to which I should turn
first, for I am powerfully drawn by the
Blood of the Son of God and by the milk
of His Virgin Mother."

St. Gertrude's writings are replete with
most beautiful sentiments concerning the

Note: Two other saintly Catholics who especially venerated the
Precious Blood were St. Gaspar del Bufalo (1786-1837) (he is
also called Caspar del Bufalo) and Mother Catherine Aurelia
of the Precious Blood (1833-1905). St. Gaspar founded
the Missioners of the Most Precious Blood in Italy; Mother

Precious Blood. To St. Mechtilde Our Lord once revealed Himself on the altar, His hands extended and **Blood streaming from His wounds.** "I show these bleeding wounds," said Jesus, "to My Father, to appease His wrath. He pardons when He sees the Blood. Let sinners but look upon Me, and they will be moved to repentance, confidence and love."

St. Catherine of Siena and St. Mary Magdalen de Pazzi practiced a very special devotion to the Precious Blood. Whenever St. Catherine of Siena, who was one of the most eminent and heroic characters in the history of the Church during the fourteenth century, thought of the Precious Blood of Jesus, the tongue of the timid virgin became eloquent, and fearlessly she stepped before kings and popes and by her zeal exercised a lasting influence on the developments of her time. Her numerous letters to bishops, cardinals and popes always began with the words: "I address you in the Precious Blood of Jesus Christ."

Catherine Aurelia founded the Sisters Adorers of the Precious Blood (in Canada). There is a monastery of her institute, along with the Confraternity of the Precious Blood, in Brooklyn, New York and another in Manchester, New Hampshire. A cause for Mother Catherine's canonization is in progress.—*Publisher,* 2008.

How to Offer the Precious Blood To the Eternal Father

One of the best means of participating in the graces and blessings of the Precious Blood is to offer it to the Eternal Father. "An offering," says Father Faber, is "more than a prayer." In prayer, we are the recipients, but when we make an offering, God deigns to accept something from us. St. Mary Magdalen de Pazzi exclaimed on one occasion when in ecstasy: "Every time a creature offers up this Blood by which he was redeemed, he offers a gift of infinite worth, which can be equaled by no other!" God revealed to this sainted Carmelite nun the practice of making this offering when He complained to her that so little effort is made in this world to **disarm His Divine justice against sinners.** Acting upon this admonition, she daily offered the Precious Blood fifty times for the living and the dead. She did this with so much fervor that God showed her on different occasions the numerous souls whose conversion she had brought about in this manner and all the Poor Souls she had delivered from Purgatory. "This devotion," says Longius, "is pleasing to God, because He is thereby honored by the best and the most sublime gifts."

Another time when St. Mary Magdalen de Pazzi was in ecstasy, she saw all the holy patrons of the city of Florence, accompanied by innumerable other Saints, before the throne of God, interceding for sinners, but their petitions remained unanswered. Then, the Guardian Angels of these poor sinners approached, but their prayers were not heard either. Next came the multitudes of the Blessed, and they made intercession for these guilty souls. While imploring God's mercy, they were intent at the same time to offer to the Eternal Father the **Precious Blood,** and on account of the merits of this Precious Blood, *their* petition was granted.

Should not these examples incite us to offer to God the Father the Precious Blood of Jesus frequently during the day?

Eternal Father, I offer Thee the Precious Blood of Jesus, in satisfaction for my sins, and for the needs of Holy Church.

By this short, efficacious prayer, an indulgence of five hundred days can be gained every time.* Many could make this offering whenever they hear the clock strike. And it is especially very efficacious when made during Mass.

In order to **obtain special graces through the Precious Blood** of Jesus Christ, let us ask the Blessed Virgin to offer it in our stead. This advice is given to us by many devout servants of God, in particular by St. John Vianney, the Curé of Ars, who says that this is the best method of prayer. Furthermore, he adds, "My children, mark this well: whenever I obtained some grace, it was obtained in this manner, which I never found to fail." In the life of St. Dominic we read that on one occasion when he was preaching about venerating Mary, he saw the Blessed Virgin sprinkling his devout hearers with the Blood of her Divine Son. Once while the Saint was celebrating Mass, three hundred persons, among them the king and queen, saw the Mother of God, at the Elevation of the Chalice, pouring the Precious Blood

---

* Partial indulgences are no longer linked to specific periods of time.—*Publisher,* 2008.

over all who were present there and over the whole Church.

Let us in particular during the Holy Sacrifice of the Mass beseech Mary to offer to the Eternal Father the Blood of her Son in the Chalice—for Holy Mother the Church, for the conversion of sinners, for the souls in Purgatory, and for all our various needs. We may enumerate them to her with full confidence, and the greater their number, the better is she pleased. What we offer to God in the Holy Sacrifice of the Mass is of infinitely greater value than what we ask for. God remains our debtor, as it were, so great is the value of the Precious Blood.

An Easy Means to Prevent Numerous Mortal Sins

Here on earth we shall never sufficiently realize what sin is. The person who sins rebels against God. It was sin which caused the death of the God-Man, Jesus Christ. Yes, sin is deicide, for according to the words of St. Bernard, "Sin murders God in so far as it is possible for man to do so." Once, when Our Lord showed St. Catherine of Genoa the heinousness of venial sin, the servant of God was so terrified that she would have died instantly had she beheld one of these stains on her own soul. "This vision," she says, "concerned only a slight fault and lasted but a moment; had it continued a little longer, it would have sufficed to cause my death, or even to change the substance of a rock into dust."

The least sin is so great an evil that the Saints say: "If we could open the gates of Hell and liberate all the souls enclosed therein, and could release all the suffering souls from Purgatory—all this by one little lie [that is, by a venial sin], we would not be permitted to do so." By preventing one *mortal* sin, we render an inestimable service to the honor of God—and how easily this can be done! Father Faber writes: "If every evening, before we retire, we would ask the Blessed Virgin Mary to offer to God the Precious Blood of her Divine Son Jesus for the intention that thereby one mortal sin which might be committed somewhere that night might be prevented, and if every morning this offering were renewed from day to day, **we could prevent many mortal sins.**" What joy and happiness this practice would bring to us! We could thereby atone for our own sins and merit immeasurable treasures for Heaven.

Here follows a striking example: St. Paphnutius (died circa 350) had for many years lived in a desert and labored at his sanctification by austere works of penance. Once a peculiar thought came to his mind, and he dared to express it to God in prayer. He petitioned the Lord, in all humility and simplicity, to reveal to him a person who had the same degree of merit as he himself. God deigned to grant his request, and He gave Paphnutius to understand that at this moment a certain flutist living in Egypt ranked equal to him in merit.

The Saint at once started on a journey to find the flutist. Having arrived at the appropriate village, and making inquiries there, he was informed that the man he was seeking was engaged at a neighboring tavern, playing for the amusement of those who patronized the place. "How strange!" thought Paphnutius. Nevertheless, he sent word to the musician, begging him for a short interview. When the musician came, the Saint took him aside and spoke to him regarding the condition of his soul. "What good deeds have you ever done?" asked Paphnutius.

"Good deeds?" replied the flutist; "I do not remember ever having done any; all I remember is that one day, while I was pursuing my former trade of stealing, I saved the honor of a virgin consecrated to God, and another time I gave my money to a poor woman who, in her great distress, was about to commit a crime." From this, our Saint realized that God had given the flutist graces similar to those he himself had received, because for the honor of his Creator, this man in his crude life had prevented two mortal sins.

You who read this, whosoever you may be, resolve to say the following little prayer every morning and evening:

O Holy and Immaculate Virgin Mary, offer to the Eternal Father the Precious Blood of thy Divine Son for the intention that one mortal sin may be prevented this day (*or* this night).

You may add a *Hail Mary* in honor of the Mother of God for this intention. Perform this devotion with great fervor and perseverance, and teach it to other devout souls. You will thereby acquire immeasurable merit.

If we truly love God, we cannot feel indifferent when God is offended. St. Mary Magdalen de Pazzi, when only eight years old, happened to hear two persons quarreling and using the most insulting language, and undoubtedly they thereby became guilty of mortal sin. The Saint was so pained at the thought of how grievously God had been offended that she spent the entire night weeping. Sixteen years had passed and she had forgotten this occurrence, when God revealed to her that in reward for the tears she had shed for the sins of others, she was destined to a special degree of glory, which was shown her in the form of a brilliant garment.

Will our reward be less if, for love of God, we try to prevent His being grievously offended? Oh, let us do our utmost, let us use every possible means, especially prayer and the offering of the Precious Blood of Jesus, to prevent mortal sins!

The Precious Blood of Jesus Extinguishes the Flames of Purgatory

The Precious Blood of Jesus is the most efficacious means to assist the suffering souls. Ah, how these Poor Souls long for one drop of the Blood of Christ! As has been mentioned, St. Mary Magdalen de Pazzi offered the Precious Blood fifty times a day, and it was revealed to her how many souls she had released. Let us follow her example and frequently during the day say the following efficacious prayer:

O Eternal Father, I offer Thee, through the Immaculate Virgin Mary, the Precious Blood of Thy Son for the relief of the suffering souls in Purgatory.

Our Lord once said to St. Mechtilde: "Through My Blood, I conquer My Father's anger and reconcile man with his God." It is especially in the Holy Sacrifice of the Mass that this Blood is being shed anew.* At one time a Poor Soul appeared to Bl.

---

* Christ's blood is "shed" in the Mass in an unbloody, mystical manner.—*Publisher,* 2008.

Henry Suso and cried out, "Blood, Blood, brother, is needed, that we may obtain relief! Masses, Masses should be said, as we have promised one another!" Once on All Souls' Day, St. John of Alverno offered the Sacred Body of Our Lord to the Heavenly Father at the Consecration and implored Him to release the souls in Purgatory through the Blood of His Divine Son. Thereupon he saw a great number of them, like sparks of fire, ascend to Heaven.

Let us make it a practice that as often as we assist at the Holy Sacrifice of the Mass, we offer to the Eternal Father the Precious Blood, by the hands of Mary, for the suffering souls in Purgatory. If we perform this act of charity for the Poor Souls, the Masses which will be said for us after our death will be far more efficacious. Anyone who during life has been heartless toward the Poor Souls may have many Masses said for himself after death, but possibly he will derive little benefit from them, for "With what measure you mete, it shall be measured to you again." (*Matthew* 7:2).

∽ *Chapter 2* ∽

The Scourging of Our Blessed Lord

A Most Painful Torture

ONE of the most painful tortures inflicted upon our Divine Saviour during His bitter Passion was the cruel Scourging at the Pillar. Our Lord beheld with vivid clearness this part of His sufferings when He "took unto him the twelve and said to them: Behold, we go up to Jerusalem, and all things shall be accomplished which were written by the prophets concerning the Son of man. For he shall be delivered to the Gentiles, and shall be mocked and scourged and spit upon. And after they have scourged him they will put him to death." (*Luke* 18:31-33). It is remarkable that *twice* Jesus mentioned here His scourging.

Many Saints have venerated our Saviour in His scourging with a special fervor. The

compassionate heart of St. Bernard melts
with pity as he contemplates the **merci-
less scourging of the Lamb of God.** St.
Alphonsus calls out to the devout soul to
be present at the scourging of Jesus and
behold the unutterable pain He endured in
atonement for our sins. But no Saint
describes so pathetically the cruel scourging of our Blessed Saviour as Blessed Anne
Catherine Emmerich. What she writes of
her vision of the scourging is capable of
moving the soul to its innermost depths.
To read her revelations is a wonderful help
for meditation on Jesus' suffering at the
scourging. We here give some excerpts:

Jesus at the Pillar
According to the revelations of
Blessed Anne Catherine Emmerich

"Pilate, the base, wavering judge, had several times pronounced the contradictory
words: "I find no cause in Him. I will chas-
tise Him, therefore, and let Him go . . .' Thereupon, while violently thrusting and beating
Jesus with short clubs, the hangmen led our
Saviour to a pillar. The executioners, throw-
ing their scourges, whips and ropes down at

the foot of the pillar, came forward to meet Jesus. They were six swarthy men who were employed for such services in the praetorium. These abominable wretches had already, at that same pillar, scourged poor sinners to death. There was something beastly, diabolical in their nature.

"Although Our Lord walked along so willingly, they **struck Him** with their fists and ropes and, **with furious rage, pulled Him** along to the scourging pillar. The pillar is just high enough for a tall person with uplifted arms to reach its upper rounded end, to which is fastened an iron ring; midway at the back of the pillar there are also rings or hooks. It is impossible to express the barbarity with which these raving men abused Jesus on this short road. They tore from Him the mock mantle of Herod and almost threw our poor Saviour to the ground.

He Prayed and Pleaded

"Jesus trembled and quivered at the sight of the pillar. In palpitating haste He Himself removed His garments with hands bleeding and swollen from tight binding, while the brutal scourgers continually struck and jerked Him about. **He prayed and pleaded so touchingly** and for a moment turned His face toward His Mother, all torn with grief. She stood with the holy women in a corner . . . near the scourging place; and He said, turning toward the pillar to cover His nakedness—as He was compelled to remove even His loincloth—'Turn thy eyes away from Me.' I do not know whether He said this outwardly or inwardly, but I perceived how Mary understood it; for I saw her that same moment, unconscious and turning aside, drop into the arms of the veiled holy women who surrounded her.

"Now **Jesus embraced the pillar,** and the hangmen, amid frightful cursing and jerking, bound His sacred hands to the iron rings behind the pillar and stretched His whole Body so far upward that His feet, which were tightly fastened to the pillar below, could scarcely touch the ground. There stood the Holy of Holies in His whole human nakedness, in **infinite anguish** and shame, stretched on the pillar of criminals, while two of the infuriated barbarians began to lash His sacred back upwards and downwards with raving bloodthirstiness.

Three Kinds of Scourges

"Their first scourges or whips appeared to be made of tough white wood; possibly too, they were of rigid oxen sinews or hard strips of white leather. Our Lord and Saviour, the Son of God, True God and true man, **twitched and writhed like a poor worm beneath the lashes** of the criminals. He moaned with pain; His clear, sweet-sounding cries, like a loving prayer amid excruciating torture, rang through the hissing blows of the hangmen's lashes . . .

"Scarcely had a quarter of an hour elapsed when the first two scourgers ceased their beating . . . The Body of Jesus was all covered with brown, blue and red stripes, and His **Sacred Blood trickled down.** He trembled and quivered. Scorn and derision resounded from all sides.

"Now the second pair of scourgers fell upon Jesus with new rage. They had different kind of whips, which were bushy, as though made of thorns, and here and there had knots and spurs fastened to them. Under the fearful lashes of these inhuman executioners, all the stripes of His sacred Body were torn open, His Blood spurted around in a circle and bespattered the arms of the hangmen. Jesus moaned and prayed and twitched in His agony.

"The next two hangmen lashed Jesus with scourges. These consisted of little chains or straps with iron hooks at the end, attached to an iron handle. With these they tore whole pieces of flesh from His ribs. Oh, who can describe the awful, shuddering sight! Still they had not enough of outrage. They loosened the cords and turned His back to the column. He was painfully drawn together, covered with Blood and Wounds. His lacerated loins and the torn skin of His Body covered His nakedness. Like furious dogs the executioners heaped blow upon blow. One of them had in his left hand a finer lash wherewith he **slashed Our Lord's face.** Not a sound spot was to be found on His Body. He turned His Blood-dimmed eyes to the executioners, pleading for mercy. But they raged the more furiously. . . . The terrible scourging lasted about three quarters of an hour . . .

"The cords which bound Jesus were cut . . . Our Saviour's lacerated frame fell in a heap on the ground at the foot of the column. . . . **Jesus lay there bathed in Blood and quivering with pain**. . . . Several times during the scourging, I saw what seemed to be mourning Angels appear around Jesus, and constantly through the piercing hail of ignominious pain, I heard Him offer Himself to God for man. And now, while He lay thus in His Blood, I saw an Angel come to refresh Him. . .

"How brutally the executioners kicked Him to get up, and made Him reach and creep so painfully for His garments, and drove Him to His feet and dragged Him past His dolorous Mother! And, O God, the sight of Our Lady as she wrung her hands and riveted her eyes on His bloody footprints! . . . His poor Mother crept near and began to **gather up so lovingly the Blood of her Son** round the column, seeking its traces wherever it had sprinkled. . ."

~ *Chapter 3* ~

The Sufferings of Our Saviour on the Cross

The Torments of the Body

WHAT our Saviour suffered on the Cross not even an Angel of Heaven could adequately describe, for His sufferings were immeasurable. Jesus on the Cross suffered two kinds of torments: **tortures of the Body and agonies of the Soul.**

The most painful tortures imaginable were inflicted upon the holy Body of Christ; it was submerged in an ocean of suffering. Through the inhuman scourging, His sacred Body was all torn and wounded. Through the brutal Crowning with Thorns, His adorable Head was pierced with numberless wounds. When Jesus was nailed to the Cross, His sacred limbs were violently extended. St. Mechtilde once asked Our Lord which was His greatest suffering on the Cross. Jesus deigned to answer: "Dreadful were the torments I experienced at the crucifixion, but **inexpressible were My tortures** when My Body was so **frightfully distended** that all My bones could be numbered. If anyone thanks Me for this suffering, he renders Me as great a service as if he had anointed all My wounds. Whoever thanks Me for the thirst I endured, I accept it from him as if he had quenched My thirst."

What martyrdom our Divine Saviour endured in His Sacred Body during those three long hours He hung upon the Cross, when every moment was an agony sufficient to cause death! The cruel nails were driven through His sacred hands and feet in the very place where all the nerves and sinews meet. But His torturous thirst was above all human comprehension.

His Anguish of Soul

Jesus is God. Through Divine assistance He endured all the evils, all the sufferings in His most holy Body and most blessed Soul. Jesus is innocent. For me He hangs on the Cross; through the Cross He reconciles me with the Father and opens Heaven for me. Oh, how I ought to love my Saviour! How I ought to thank Him!

The greatest suffering of His Soul was that He was **forsaken by His Heavenly Father.** Had God deigned to cast but one compassionate look upon the Soul of Jesus, He would have been comforted. The Soul of Jesus found in God only inexorable rigor and justice. Jesus alone can fully comprehend all the torture His Sacred Humanity endured in His dereliction on the Cross.

What a suffering must it have been for the loving Heart of the Son to see His holy, sinless **Mother at the foot of the Cross,** her soul overwhelmed in an ocean of grief and compassion; to see her heart pierced by the "sword of sorrow"!

How cruelly bitter was the anguish of His Heart at the thought that His death on the Cross would be suffered in vain for the greater part of mankind, and that many would even curse Him, all of whom He wished to redeem and save!

"Had this sorrow been something material, neither the distance between Heaven and earth, nor the immensity of the universe would be capable of containing it," writes a soul privileged by God.

Alas, we think too little of the sufferings of the Body and the holy Soul of Jesus when we look at the crucifix! What an **awful thing sin must be,** that the God-Man had to suffer thus to expiate it! Nothing preaches the justice of God more impressively than the bitter Passion and Death of Jesus Christ.

What Does Our Saviour Say to Us from the Cross?

The image of the Crucified shows us not only the justice of God, but also, and even more, His infinite love for man. This Our Lord revealed to St. Gertrude as she one day affectionately held her crucifix and kissed it. "Every time one kisses the crucifix," said Jesus, "or looks at it with devotion, the eye of God's mercy is fixed upon his soul. He should then listen within himself to these words of tenderness from Me: 'Behold how I, for love of thee, hang on the Cross—naked, despised, My whole Body wounded, all My limbs distended. And still My Heart is enkindled with such glowing love for thee, that if it were beneficial for thy salvation and thou couldst not be saved in any other way, I would for thee alone endure all that I suffered for the whole world.'"

Through such meditation man is incited to gratitude, for it is always a great grace when one looks lovingly at an image of the Crucified; while, on the contrary, a disregard for this precious sign of our Redemption would bring sad spiritual losses. Another time, the same Saint, while lovingly contemplating the image of the Crucified, understood that "When anyone, with tender devotion, looks upon this image, **Our Lord** in turn **looks upon him** with such merciful compassion that his soul receives a most consoling impression from Divine Love, so that the whole Heavenly Court is filled with joy. The oftener he does this on earth with reverence and love, the greater will be his reward in Heaven."

Is this not a most consoling promise, capable to incite us to look very often with love and devotion upon our Crucified Saviour!

Our Sins and Negligences

The remembrance of the bitter Passion and ignominious death of Jesus Christ is an **unspeakable comfort** when we are weighed down by the thought of **our many sins and negligences.** Meditation on the Passion is an effective remedy against sin. This also Our Lord revealed to His beloved St. Gertrude. "If a person laden with grievous sins were to offer to God My sufferings and My death, which I endured innocently, he would uplift himself through this hope, so that his sins would be forgiven; yea, in virtue of this act he would even receive the remission of the temporal punishment, for there is **no remedy more effective against sin** than the **devout remembrance of My Passion,** connected with a true spirit of penance."

On a certain Friday evening, St. Gertrude cast her eyes on a crucifix, and penetrated with grief, she exclaimed: "Ah, my Beloved, what cruelties Thou hast suffered on this day for my salvation! And I, alas, have been so occupied that I have not devoutly recalled what Thou didst suffer for me each hour . . . when Thou didst **die for love of me!"**

From the Cross, Our Lord answered: "I have **supplied** what thou hast neglected, for I have accumulated each hour in My Heart what thou oughtest to have accumulated in thy heart; consequently, My Heart is so inflamed with love that I have ardently desired this hour in which thou wouldst address this prayer to Me, in union with which I will offer to God My Father all I have done for thee during this day, and without which thy contrition could not be so advantageous for thy salvation." From this we learn the faithful love of Jesus toward man and how He Himself makes atonement for our faults and negligences if we are sorry for them. Let us offer to the Heavenly Father our Crucified Lord, bleeding from every wound, in expiation for our sins. The Eternal Father cannot refuse us forgiveness when He beholds His dearly beloved Son making such complete atonement for our offenses. Oh, how consoling it is that we have an all-powerful Mediator before the Father! To represent to ourselves **our Saviour, suffering so cruelly for our sins,** is the best means to awaken in our hearts sentiments of perfect contrition. Oh, how profitable it is for souls to kneel frequently before a crucifix and awaken sorrow for their sins! Then they too will receive the sweet reward accorded to St. Gertrude.

Devotion to the Five Holy Wounds

Even after His Resurrection, our Divine Saviour **retained the five Wounds in His Sacred Body.** He shows these glorious Wounds to the Eternal Father in Heaven and pleads for our salvation. He also desires these holy Wounds to be venerated in a special manner by the faithful of His Church. Many Saints had great devotion to the Five Holy Wounds and kissed them a countless number of times on the crucifix. This practice is very pleasing to God, and He has often rewarded it with signal graces. Only think of the privileged souls who were favored to bear the sacred stigmata in their own body; all these were specially devoted to the suffering Saviour.

St. Gertrude declares that she never failed to receive some new favor each time she applied herself in spirit to venerate the adorable Wounds of Jesus. Our Lord Himself taught her to say this prayer while saluting His holy Wounds:

Hail, Jesus, my most loving Saviour! I salute Thee in the ineffable joys of Thy Divinity; I embrace Thee with the affection of the whole creation, and I kiss the sacred Wounds of Thy love.

Our Saviour assured St. Gertrude that if one recites these words in honor of His Five Holy Wounds, while kissing them devoutly and adding some prayers or good works, and offering them through His sweetest Heart, **they will be as acceptable to God as the most arduous devotion.**

Another efficacious practice in honor of the Five Holy Wounds is to pray the *Our Father* five times with extended arms. According to Bl. Anne Catherine Emmerich, the Heavenly Father cannot reject such a prayer because He is thereby reminded of His Son hanging on the Cross.

St. Gertrude was accustomed to kiss the Five Holy Wounds in expiation for her sins. When she kissed the wound in the left foot, she obtained the full remission of all her **sins in thoughts and words.** Through the wound in the right foot, Jesus supplied all her **omissions in holy thoughts and words.** Through the wound in the left hand, He granted her the remission of all **sinful deeds.** Through the wound in the right hand, He supplied all her **omissions**

in good works. Through the wound in His sacred side, she was **cleansed from every sin** by those precious drops of Blood and water which were shed from the opening made by the lance. Through the Precious Blood shed from the Five Wounds, she was adorned with every virtue. Is not this a meritorious practice! It should induce pious souls to kiss the Five Holy Wounds frequently.

∽ *Chapter 4* ∽

The Crucifix

THE Cross is the sign of our Redemption. We revere it, salute it, and while venerating it, we adore our Blessed Lord who died upon it for our salvation. No image is so widely circulated in Christendom and so highly venerated in the Catholic Church as the crucifix. Every altar upon which a priest offers the Adorable Sacrifice must have a cross, and the Sign of the Cross is used at all the consecrations of Holy Church. Every truly Christian family holds the **crucifix as the most treasured ornament of the home.** How touching is the custom for the bride or bridegroom to bring to their new home a beautiful crucifix* and give it an honored

---

* It is very difficult, in fact, well-nigh impossible to secure a crucifix with expressive features of our suffering Saviour. We recommend for every home a beautiful enlarged picture of the Holy Christ of Limpias. No words can express its grandeur and beauty and the depth of impression this picture makes on one who studies it. Much more so than a crucifix, it

33

place! This is proof that Jesus Christ
Crucified is the true Lord of the house.

What silent sermons are given by a worthy image of our Crucified Saviour! From
its place it urges the family to have their
hearts animated by Christian sentiments.
It looks down so earnestly when the members of the family enjoy happiness and pros-
perity, and so mildly and consolingly when
they suffer misfortune. From its quiet place,
the **crucifix preaches** of grace, of forgiveness, of patience and of charity; it
warns and admonishes family members so
mildly when some of them go astray on the
way of sin. When disunion disturbs the
peace and tranquility of the home, then
from the silent lips of the Crucified Lamb
who hangs on the wall come touching admo-
nitions for forgiveness and reconciliation.

O Christian families, honor and venerate the crucifix! **Jesus Crucified is your
true friend,** the witness of all that hap-
pens in your family. How quickly the days
and weeks pass, but He is always in your
midst. He sees your children grow to matu-
rity; He sees how loved ones are carried

---

presents to us the bitter sufferings and merciful love of our
Blessed Lord. *(Author's note, 1926.)*

from your home in the coffin; He sees you in your happiness, and again He gazes upon you when your eyes are wet with tears. He is your only true consoler, ever near to comfort you. Jesus has said: "And I, if I be lifted up from the earth, will draw all things to myself." (*John* 12:32). Oh, may the image of the Crucified Saviour draw the hearts of all members of the family to Himself, unite them in prayer and in charity, keep them from the vanities of the world and be the source of mutual love.

Union with Jesus Crucified

The crucifix is in truth a school of all virtues. Our Divine Saviour taught St. Gertrude how we should look up to Him as our model in our sufferings. When we hear our dying Saviour pray for His enemies and excuse them before His Father, "Father, forgive them, for they know not what they do" (*Luke* 23:34), should it then not be easy for us to love our enemies? In union with that love with which Jesus prayed for His enemies, we too should pray for those who injure us. One day when St. Gertrude prayed thus for her enemies, Our Lord was so pleased that He granted her the forgiveness of all her sins.

St. Gertrude likewise understood the value and meritoriousness of all that is done in union with the Passion of Christ. If we have anything to suffer, let us think or say:

O Jesus, in union with that love wherewith Thou didst suffer for me, I will suffer this and offer it to Thee. I place my sufferings in Thy love-glowing Heart; grant that they may obtain the conversion of sinners, perseverance for the just, and help and consolation for the Poor Souls.

∽Chapter 5∽

Prayers

Litany in Honor of the Precious Blood

(For private use only.)

Lord, have mercy on us.
  Christ, have mercy on us.
Lord, have mercy on us. Christ, hear us.
  Christ, graciously hear us.
God the Father of Heaven,
  Have mercy on us.
God the Son, Redeemer of the world,
  Have mercy on us.
God the Holy Ghost,
  Have mercy on us.
Holy Trinity, one God,
  Have mercy on us.

Blood of Jesus, the Son of the Eternal
  Father, *Cleanse us, O Precious Blood!*

Note: We have added to this booklet an additional litany to the Precious Blood—one which was approved for public use by Pope John XXIII in 1960. (See p. 42). There are only six litanies approved for public use.—*Publisher,* 2008.

Blood of Jesus, formed by the Holy Ghost
in the heart of the Virgin Mother,
Cleanse us, O Precious Blood!

Blood of Jesus, substantially united to the
Word of God, *etc.*

Blood of Jesus, of infinite majesty,

Blood of Jesus, of infinite worth,

Blood of Jesus, shed in the circumcision,

Blood of Jesus, shed in the agony on
Mount Olivet,

Blood of Jesus, shed in the scourging,

Blood of Jesus, shed in the crowning of
thorns,

Blood of Jesus, shed on the Way of the
Cross,

Blood of Jesus, shed at the crucifixion,

Blood of Jesus, shed at the opening of
the Sacred Side,

Blood of Jesus, shed in love for mankind,

Blood of Jesus, shed in obedience to the
Father,

Blood of Jesus, Sacrifice to Divine Justice,

Blood of Jesus, memorial of the bitter
Passion,

Blood of Jesus, seal of the New and
Eternal Testament,

Blood of Jesus, which formed the Church,
our Mother,

Blood of Jesus, which ransomed us from the slavery of Satan,

Blood of Jesus, which reopened Heaven for us,

Blood of Jesus, which cries more loudly than the blood of Abel,

Blood of Jesus, which pacifies the wrath of the Father,

Blood of Jesus, which mitigates or averts punishments,

Blood of Jesus, propitiation for our sins,

Blood of Jesus, cleansing bath for the sinful soul,

Blood of Jesus, balsam for the wounds of the soul,

Blood of Jesus, source of peace and reconciliation,

Blood of Jesus, flowing in the Eucharistic Heart,

Blood of Jesus, imploring grace for us,

Blood of Jesus, flowing mystically in the Holy Sacrifice,

Blood of Jesus, inebriating drink of the children of God,

Blood of Jesus, healing drink of the sick and weak,

Blood of Jesus, refreshing drink of the banished children of Eve,

Blood of Jesus, love-potion of God-loving
  souls,
Blood of Jesus, celestial wine of virgins,
Blood of Jesus, source of all consolation,
Blood of Jesus, source of love and mercy,
Blood of Jesus, source of life and holiness,
Blood of Jesus, medicine of immortality,
Blood of Jesus, reviled and despised,
Blood of Jesus, worthy of all praise,
Blood of Jesus, comfort of the patriarchs,
Blood of Jesus, desire of the prophets,
Blood of Jesus, power and strength of the
  Apostles and martyrs,
Blood of Jesus, sanctification of virgins
  and confessors,
Blood of Jesus, terror of evil spirits,
Blood of Jesus, salvation of those who
  trust in Thee,
Blood of Jesus, hope of those who die in
  Thee,
Blood of Jesus, consolation and refresh-
  ment of the Poor Souls,
Blood of Jesus, key of Heaven,
Blood of Jesus, pledge of eternal
  blessedness,
Blood of Jesus, delight of all the Saints,
Blood of Jesus, the Lamb without spot or
  blemish,

Lamb of God, Who takest away the sins
of the world,
Spare us, O Lord!
Lamb of God, Who takest away the sins
of the world,
Graciously hear us, O Lord!
Lamb of God, Who takest away the sins
of the world,
Have mercy on us, O Lord!

V. Thou hast redeemed us, O Lord, in Thy
Blood,
R. *And hast made us a kingdom to our
God.*

Let Us Pray

Almighty and Eternal God, Who hast
given Thine only-begotten Son as a Saviour to the world and Who didst will to be
reconciled by His Blood, grant us, we
beseech Thee, the grace so to honor the
Price of our Salvation, and through its
power to be protected against all the evils
of the present life, that we may enjoy the
fruit thereof in Heaven. Through Jesus
Christ, Our Lord, who liveth and reigneth
with Thee in the unity of the Holy Spirit,
God, world without end. Amen.

Litany of the
Most Precious Blood of Jesus

(For public or private use.)

Lord, have mercy on us.
  Christ, have mercy on us.
Lord, have mercy on us. Christ, hear us.
  Christ, graciously hear us.
God the Father of Heaven,
  Have mercy on us.
God the Son, Redeemer of the world,
  Have mercy on us.
God the Holy Spirit,
  Have mercy on us.
Holy Trinity, one God,
  Have mercy on us.

Blood of Christ, only-begotten Son of the
  Eternal Father, *save us.*
Blood of Christ, Incarnate Word of God,
  save us.
Blood of Christ, of the New and Eternal
  Testament, *etc.*
Blood of Christ, falling upon the earth in
  the Agony,
Blood of Christ, shed profusely in the
  Scourging,
Blood of Christ, flowing forth in the
  Crowning with Thorns,

Blood of Christ, poured out on the Cross,

Blood of Christ, Price of our Salvation,

Blood of Christ, without which there is
no forgiveness,

Blood of Christ, Eucharistic Drink and
Refreshment of Souls,

Blood of Christ, River of Mercy,

Blood of Christ, Victor over Demons,

Blood of Christ, Courage of Martyrs,

Blood of Christ, Strength of Confessors,

Blood of Christ, bringing forth virgins,

Blood of Christ, Help of those in Peril,

Blood of Christ, Relief of the Burdened,

Blood of Christ, Solace in Sorrow,

Blood of Christ, Hope of the Penitent,

Blood of Christ, Consolation of the Dying,

Blood of Christ, Peace and Tenderness of
Hearts,

Blood of Christ, Pledge of Eternal Life,

Blood of Christ, freeing souls from
Purgatory,

Blood of Christ, most worthy of all glory
and honor,

Lamb of God, Who takest away the sins
of the world,
Spare us, O Lord.

Lamb of God, Who takest away the sins

of the world,
Graciously hear us, O Lord.
Lamb of God, Who takest away the sins
of the world,
Have mercy on us.

V. Thou hast redeemed us, O Lord, in Thy
Blood,
R. *And made of us a kingdom for our God.*

Let Us Pray

Almighty and Eternal God, Thou hast
appointed Thine only-begotten Son the Redeemer of the world and willed to be ap-
peased by His Blood. Grant, we beseech
Thee, that we may worthily adore this Price
of our Salvation, and through its power be
safeguarded from the evils of this present
life, so that we may rejoice in its fruits for-
ever in Heaven. Through the same Christ
Our Lord. R. *Amen.*

Imprimatur: ✠ Joseph V. Sullivan, S.T.D.
Bishop of Baton Rouge

Invocations to the
Precious Blood of Jesus

PRECIOUS Blood of Jesus, shed in the Circumcision, make me chaste of mind, heart and body.

Precious Blood, oozing from every pore in the Agony of Jesus, grant me to love above all things the holy and Adorable Will of God.

Precious Blood, flowing abundantly in the Scourging at the Pillar, inspire me with a keen sorrow for my sins and a love of suffering.

Precious Blood, falling in profusion from the Crown of Thorns, grant me a love of humiliations.

Precious Blood, furrowing the way to Calvary, fill me with courage to walk unfalteringly in the bloody footsteps of Jesus.

Precious Blood, shed so profusely in the Crucifixion of my Jesus, make me die entirely to self-love.

Precious Blood, shed to the very last drop by the opening of the Sacred Heart of Jesus, give me that generous love that sacrifices all for God.

Precious Blood, sacred source from

whence flow all graces, apply Thine infinite merits to my soul.

Precious Blood, Whose virtue animates and vivifies our actions, apply Thine infinite merits to all our works.

Life-Giving Fountain, in which the soul fully slakes its thirst, saturate me with pure love.

O Divine Blood of my Jesus, I adore Thee from the depths of my heart. Thee I fervently invoke, for Thou art my salvation, and by Thee I hope to obtain the joys of Paradise.

Eternal Father, be merciful, for the sake of the Blood of Thine only-begotten Son; we beseech Thee, show us Thy mercy.

Most Precious Blood of Jesus, cry to the Heavenly Father for mercy for us, and deliver us.

Eternal Father, I offer Thee the Precious Blood of Jesus in atonement for my sins and for the needs of Holy Church.

A Precious Offering through the Blessed Virgin Mary

St. John Vianney, the Curé of Ars, that prodigy of holiness in the 19th Century, was accustomed in special necessities to offer to the Eternal Father, by the hands of Mary, our Divine Saviour all covered with Blood and Wounds. This, he said, was an infallible means to obtain the most precious graces. Do you, O Christian Soul, likewise adopt this practice, and frequently repeat this offering most fervently.

O MARY, Mother of Sorrows, I beseech thee, by the inexpressible tortures thou didst endure at the death of thy Son, offer to the Eternal Father, in my place, thy beloved Son all covered with Blood and Wounds, for the grace of . . . Amen.

Prayer in Honor of the Scourging of Our Lord

"THEN Pilate took Jesus and scourged Him." O Jesus, my Bridegroom, Thou glory of Heaven, my heart is torn with sorrow as I behold Thee delivered into the hands of infamous wretches!

O humiliation of my Redeemer, I see how Thou dost give power and permission to these criminals to bruise most unmercifully

Thy pure, virginal Body, and to shed Thy Precious Blood!

Come, O ye Angels of Heaven, be present at this painful scene! And if it is not granted you to deliver your King from the cruel maltreatment of man, come at least to weep over Him!

Beloved Jesus, Thy garments are roughly torn from Thee. Bowing Thy head and blushing from shame, Thou dost await this frightful torture. Now the fiendish executioners pounce upon Thee, O innocent Lamb of God!

This one strikes Thy back, another Thy side, and another Thy limbs. Ah, already Thy Sacred Body is one wound; already Thy Precious Blood stains the scourges and the arms of the hangmen; already it besprinkles the pillar and ground.

Stroke after stroke, lash after lash, cuts and mangles Thine immaculate flesh, O innocent Jesus, and Thy sacred Blood flows in streams.

Now they turn Thee around and strike Thy breast, Thy whole sacred Body; yea, even Thine adorable head; Thy beautiful countenance is not spared from blows.

O Thou Joy of Angels, Thou Bliss of the

Elect, who could treat Thee so inhumanly? Who has so cruelly lacerated Thee, O virginal flesh! Alas, it is I! Thou dost suffer the punishment due to my sins.

O Son of God, Thou great Lover of my soul, how is it possible that Thou, O Lord of Infinite Majesty, couldst so much love me, a despicable creature, that Thou wouldst for me submit to the agonizing tortures of the scourging?

God is scourged for me! In expiation for my sins, He is crushed and wounded, torn and mangled from head to foot, so that there remains no sound spot on His sacred Body!

O guiltless Jesus, never will I belong to those who look with indifference upon their God torn with scourges. I will compassionate Thy sufferings, my Saviour; I will reflect on the boundless love with which my most loving Redeemer endured these untold tortures for love of me.

Hail, loving Jesus! I venerate the cruel Wounds and Sacred Blood of Thy most painful scourging. To Thee be all praise, all thanksgiving, and all love, for evermore!

V. He was wounded for our iniquities.

R. *He was bruised for our sins.*

Let Us Pray

I adore Thee most profoundly, O insulted Saviour, suffering such great ignominy at the pillar of scourging. Pardon me and wash away my sins in Thy Blood. I detest them because by them I have scourged Thee and insulted Thine infinite goodness. Preserve me, I beseech Thee, from every sin against holy purity; sanctify my soul and body, that I may be a living temple of the Holy Spirit, Thou Who livest and reignest world without end. *Amen.*

A Very Useful Manner of Hiding Oneself in the Five Sacred Wounds

This was taught to St. Mechtilde by Christ Himself as she went to kiss the Cross one Good Friday. (Book 1, ch. 23 and 29).

I THANK Thee, O Lord Jesus Christ, for the painful *Wound of Thy left foot,* from which flowed the Precious Blood that washes away our sins. In it I sink and hide all the sins I have ever committed. *Amen.*

I thank Thee, O Lord Jesus Christ, for the painful *Wound of Thy right foot,* from

which the fountain of peace flowed to us.
In its depths I sink and bury all my desires,
that they may be purified and remain
unspotted by any earthly stain. *Amen.*

I thank Thee, O Lord Jesus Christ, for
the painful *Wound of Thy left hand,* from
which the well of grace flowed to us. In it
I enclose all my spiritual and bodily ills,
that in union with Thy sufferings they may
become sweet to me, and by patience
become a fragrant odor before God. *Amen.*

I thank Thee, O Lord Jesus Christ, for
the painful *Wound of Thy right hand,* from
which the medicine of the soul was poured
forth. In it I hide all my negligences and
omissions which I have committed in my
virtuous exercises, that they may be atoned
for by Thy zealous works. *Amen.*

I thank Thee, O Lord Jesus Christ, for
the healing *Wound of Thy sweetest Heart,*
from which living Water and Blood and the
riches of all good flowed to us. I place
myself in this Wound, and there unite all
my imperfect love to Thy divine love, that
thus it may be perfected. *Amen.*

Five Hymns of Praise in Honor Of the Sufferings of Christ

O MOST gentle Jesus, I praise and bless Thine incomprehensible power, which became weak and helpless for us in Thy Passion.

O most patient Jesus, I praise and bless Thine inscrutable wisdom, in which Thou, while suffering for us, didst submit to be treated as a fool.

O most afflicted Jesus, I praise and bless Thine inexpressible love, in which Thou, while suffering innocently for mankind, wast hated by them.

O most sorrowful Jesus, I praise and bless Thy most beneficent mercy, in which Thou, while suffering for us, wast sentenced to a most cruel death.

O forsaken Jesus, I praise and bless Thy most loving sweetness, in which Thou, while suffering for us, didst endure a most bitter death.

O dearest Jesus, I beseech Thee to offer to Thy Father all the injustice done to Thee in Thy suffering, to His eternal praise and glory and for our salvation. *Amen.*

Three Acts of Thanksgiving to Jesus on the Cross

St. Mechtilde once asked Our Lord which had been His greatest suffering. Our Lord replied: "The forcible stretching out upon the Cross, so that all My bones might have been numbered; and if anyone shall give Me special thanks for this suffering, it shall be as though he anointed My wounds with fragrant ointment. And if anyone shall give Me thanks for the thirst I suffered, it shall be as though he had allayed that thirst in My Passion. Moreover, if he shall give Me thanks that I willed to be fastened to My Cross with nails, it shall be as acceptable to Me as though he had taken Me down from it."

O MOST meek and gentle Lamb of God, Who during three long hours didst hang so piteously upon the Cross, with the affection of all Thy creatures I give Thee thanks for that intolerable pain Thou didst endure when Thou wast so cruelly stretched out upon the Cross that all Thy bones might have been numbered. I beseech Thee, by that pain, to forgive me all the sins which I have ever committed against Thee with any member of my body.

O most innocent Lamb of God, with the gratitude of every creature of Thy hands, I give Thee thanks for the burning thirst Thou didst suffer for the salvation of the world, when with plaintive voice Thou didst exclaim: "I thirst!" And still, nothing was given Thee to drink but vinegar and gall. I beseech Thee by the bitterness of that thirst, to forgive me all the sins which I have committed against Thee by immoderate eating and drinking.

O most meek Lamb of God, with the mutual gratitude of the three Persons of the Adorable Trinity, I give Thee thanks for the dreadful anguish Thou didst endure when Thou wast so pitilessly fastened to the Cross with iron nails driven through Thy sacred hands and feet, so that Thy Heart shuddered and Thy whole frame quivered with agony. By this Thy cruel pain and by Thy most bitter death, I beseech Thee to wash away the sinful actions of my hands and feet, and to appease Thy Father's wrath against me by showing to Him Thy most Sacred Wounds. *Amen.*

Prayer to the Heavenly Father

O MOST loving Father, in union with that love wherewith Thy Son offered Himself once upon the Cross and now offers Himself to Thee upon the altar, I offer Him to Thee for the welfare and salvation of Thy whole Church.

Look upon His virginal flesh so cruelly torn by the scourges, bruised with blows and buffetings, defiled with spittle, covered with Blood, pierced with sharp thorns, swollen and livid with stripes, torn by the nails and pierced by the lance. May that pity which drew Him down from Heaven and sweetly constrained Him to immolate Himself upon the Cross, and now constrains Him to offer Himself daily to Thee upon the altar, move Thee now, O Heavenly Father, to have mercy on us. *Amen.*

Offering of the Precious Blood
From *The Raccolta.*

ETERNAL Father, I offer Thee the most Precious Blood of Jesus Christ in atonement for my sins, and in supplication for the holy souls in Purgatory and for the needs of Holy Church.

To Prevent One Mortal Sin

O HOLY and Immaculate Virgin Mary, offer to the Eternal Father the Precious Blood of thy Divine Son for the intention that one mortal sin may be prevented this day (*or* this night).

Offering of the Precious Blood
Through Our Lady
For the Souls in Purgatory

O ETERNAL Father, I offer Thee, through the Immaculate Virgin Mary, the Precious Blood of Thy Son for the relief of the suffering souls in Purgatory.

———————

July 1 is the Feast of the Precious Blood (in the traditional liturgical calendar). July is the month of the Precious Blood.